WHILE SOME OF THESE RECIPES CALL FOR E
FUN IDEAS FOR GREAT FLAVOR COMBINATI
TO ADJUST THE INGREDIENTS TO SUIT YO\

M000106819

SUMMER
"Sugar-Meets-Salt"
Salad

toss it all together... drizzle with olive oil

add a splash of fresh lime juice

4 ripe tomatoes
(variety of colors)

2 ears fresh corn
(grilled + sliced off cob)

4 ripe peaches
(pitted and cut into wedges)

1/2 cup red onion
(thinly sliced)

3/4 cup feta cheese
(cubed)

1 cup croutons
(preferably homemade)

Pomegranate
Pear

MâCHE
BiG SHâViNGS of PARMESâN
WâLnuT SâLâD

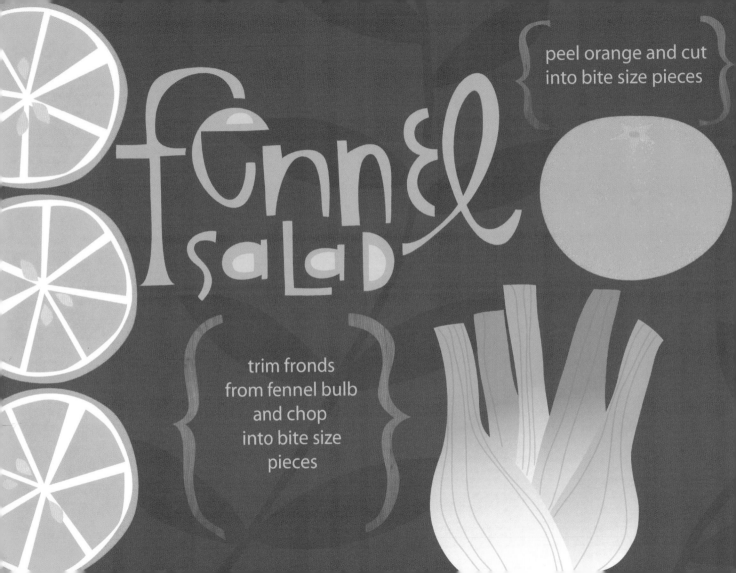

fennel salad

peel orange and cut into bite size pieces

trim fronds from fennel bulb and chop into bite size pieces

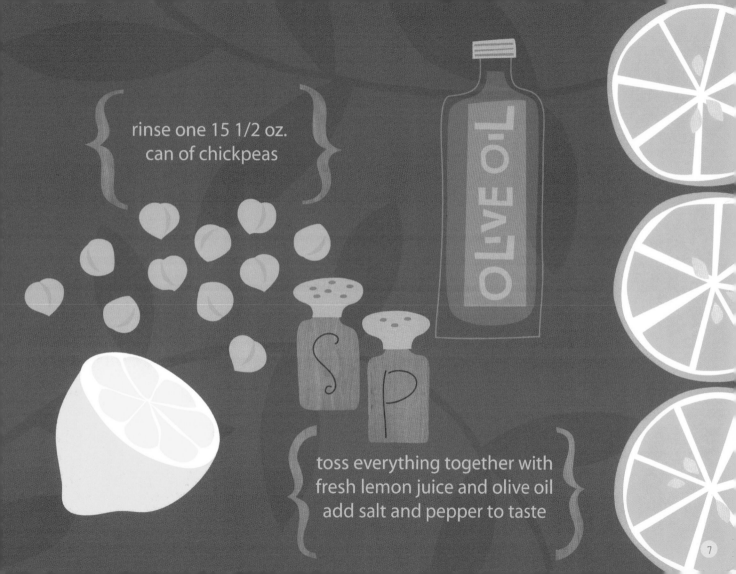

rinse one 15 1/2 oz.
can of chickpeas

OLIVE OIL

S P

toss everything together with
fresh lemon juice and olive oil
add salt and pepper to taste

avoCADos saLad

OLIVE

ONE ORANGE CUT INTO BITE SIZE PIECES
12 OUNCE BAG OF FRESH CRANBERRIES
ONE CARROT THINLY SLICED
ONE CUP OF WATER
1/2 CUP OF SUGAR
1/2 tsp. CINNAMON
1/4 tsp. NUTMEG

COMBINE ALL INGREDIENTS
IN SAUCEPAN & BRING TO BOIL

CONTINUE BOILING FOR 3 MINUTES

REDUCE HEAT & SIMMER 10 MORE MINUTES

LET SIT FOR 20 MINUTES - STORE IN REFRIGERATOR

SERVE OVER YOGURT

SPRINKLE WITH PISTACHIOS

CRANBERRY-DELUXE

PERFECT TO SERVE WHEN GUESTS ARE IN TOWN

SUPER SALSA

1 red pepper
diced

1 yellow pepper
diced

2 chopped
kumato
tomatoes

1/2 cup diced
kalamata olives

1/2 red onion
diced

salt
+
pepper
to taste

1 tbsp
lime juice

2 cups
cooked quinoa

1/2
bunch
chopped
cilantro

MIX
together
serve with
blue
corn chips

1 tbsp
chili
powder

13

CHICK PEA

DIP

LEMON OLIVE OIL

MINT PARSLEY

1/2 cup olive oil
1 chopped onion
4 small garlic cloves
2 cups rinsed chick peas
1/3 cup fresh mint, chopped
1/4 cup fresh parsley, chopped
2 TBS + 1 tsp fresh lemon juice
S + P

*serve with crackers
+ carrots

heat 1/2 of the oil in pan — medium heat
*add onion ... cook til softened
*add garlic cook 2 minutes
*add chickpeas + cook 3 minutes
let cool 15 minutes
*add chickpea mixture, mint, parsley
+ lemon juice to food processor ... puree
add s + p... stream in remaining oil

YUM!

tomAT• BaSil Kabobs

OLIVE OIL

S P

8–10 redskin potatoes
{scrubbed + quartered}

about 2 carrots
{peeled + diced}

1 cup of cooked peas

2 green onions
{thinly sliced}

1/8 cup fresh mint
{finely chopped}

SPRINGTIME FRESH POTATOES

cook potatoes til tender
{let cool}

✤

toss with other ingredients
{gently}

✤

drizzle with olive oil + lemon juice
{salt and pepper to taste}

BUTTER
BEANS
WiTH
MiNT

OLIVE OIL

S

1 15 oz. can BUTTER BEANS
(rinsed + drained)

1/4 small Red oNioN
(thinly sliced)

2 TBS. FResh MinT
(large leaves torn)

1 TBS. minced jaLapeño

1/2 tsp. Fresh Lemon juice

1/2 tsp. Lemon zest

3 TBS. oLive oiL

Toss it all
togeTHeR
+
SeasoN with
Salt + PePPeR
(Let Stand 20 min.)

ooooh... NoW CRUMBle
some FeTa CHeese oN Top !!!

Veggies

* slice 'em and dice 'em
* toss with olive oil, S + P
* bundle 'em in tin foil
* place on grill for about 10-15 minutes
* mix with couscous or quinoa
* sprinkle with big shavings of parmesan
* for extra zip add some red pepper flakes
* yum!

2 tbs. canola oil
1 sm. chopped yellow onion
2 cloves finely chopped garlic
1 tbs. chopped fresh ginger
1 seeded, finely chopped jalapeño chile
1 tbs. curry powder
salt & pepper
1 lg. peeled & cubed sweet potato (1/2 inch)
1 can 15 oz. drained & rinsed chick peas
1 can 14 oz. coconut milk
1/2 cup frozen peas
1/2 cup drained canned diced tomatoes
steamed basmati rice

curry

make curry base~
*warm oil in saucepan
*add onion, garlic, ginger & chile
*cook about 4 minutes
*stir in curry & cook 30 seconds
*season with salt & pepper

cook vegetables~
*add sweet potato, chick peas, coconut milk, &
  1 cup water to curry saucepan
*raise heat to medium-high, bring to boil, reduce
  heat & simmer, uncovered, until sweet potato is
  tender, about 10 minutes
*add peas & tomatoes & cook until heated
  through
*serve in bowls over steamed rice

slice 1 large sweet potato into thin wedges

toss with olive oil, fresh thyme, S + P

spread single layer on baking sheet

roast for 20 minutes at 425°

sauté small chopped onion in olive oil...
stir in 1 can of black beans (rinsed)

once everything is cooked
layer them on your
favorite plate...
rice
*
sweet potatoes
*
beans

cook rice according to package

FENNEL

THYME

SPINACH

MUSHROOMS

SWEET PEPPERS

CHILE
FLAKES
ONION

ROSEMARY

Sauté + Serve

...really yummy over basmati rice...

SAUTÉ

garlic

leeks

shitake mushrooms

cauliflower

sun—dried
tomatoes
packed in oil

OLIVE
OIL

salt + pepper
to taste

grill pineapple slices...

your favorite
soft white cheese...
thinly sliced

{ I like Havarti }

slice in half...

PINEAPPLE
GRILLED CHEESE

rustic french bread. . . butter one side

spicy brown mustard

Layer GRILL + ENJOY

a few fresh thyme leaves

33

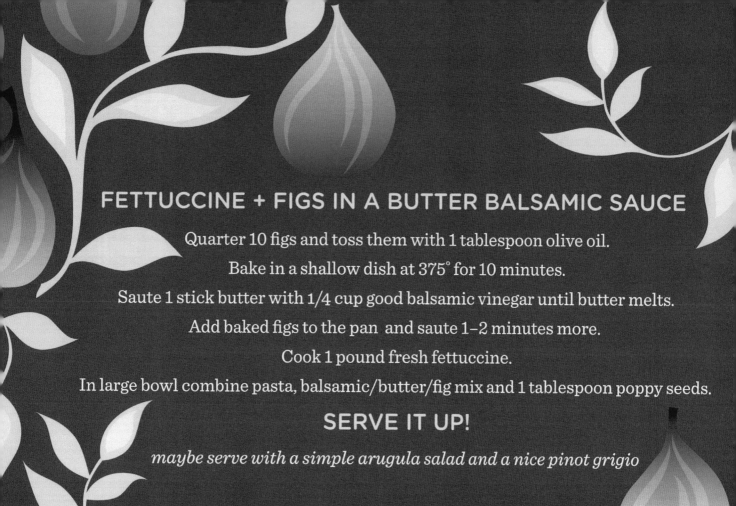

FETTUCCINE + FIGS IN A BUTTER BALSAMIC SAUCE

Quarter 10 figs and toss them with 1 tablespoon olive oil.

Bake in a shallow dish at 375° for 10 minutes.

Saute 1 stick butter with 1/4 cup good balsamic vinegar until butter melts.

Add baked figs to the pan and saute 1–2 minutes more.

Cook 1 pound fresh fettuccine.

In large bowl combine pasta, balsamic/butter/fig mix and 1 tablespoon poppy seeds.

SERVE IT UP!

maybe serve with a simple arugula salad and a nice pinot grigio

ROASTED BUTTERNUT SQUASH PIZZA

1

PEEL SQUASH AND CUT INTO 1/8 INCH SLICES

*

THINLY SLICE ONE LARGE SHALLOT

*

FINELY CHOP 2 SPRIGS OF ROSEMARY

*

TOSS ALL WITH 2 TBS. OLIVE OIL SALT + PEPPER

*

ARRANGE IN SINGLE LAYER ON A BAKING SHEET

BAKE AT 400° FOR 25 MINUTES

2

TOAST 1/2 CUP OF PINE NUTS

3 BRING OVEN TO 450°
ROLL OUT 16 OZ. REFRIGERATED
PIZZA DOUGH ON BAKING SHEET
*
TOP WITH SQUASH MIXTURE
BAKE FOR 13-17 MINUTES
(CRISPY CRUST)

4 DRIZZLE PIZZA WITH
OLIVE OIL & TOP WITH
HANDFULS OF SPINACH
*
PINE NUTS
*
BIG SHAVINGS OF
PARMESAN

carrots

berries

spinach

sunflower seeds

mangoes

tea

water

avocados

recipe for healthy skin

sweet

potatoes

kiwi

tomatoes

pour
coffee
over
crushed
cardamom

brew
your
favorite
coffee
(preferably dark roast, french press)

crush 2
cardamom pods
at the bottom of your
coffee cup (not too fine)

coffee

enjoy!

add
cream
or
sugar
or
both

41

COMBINE IN A LARGE SAUCEPAN & BRING TO A BOIL
{SIMMER OVER LOW HEAT FOR 10 MINUTES}

4 CUPS OF APPLE CIDER
BOTTLE OF ITALIAN RED WINE
1/4 CUP HONEY
2 CINNAMON STICKS
4 WHOLE CLOVES
1 BAY LEAF
1 ORANGE, ZESTED AND JUICED
1 VANILLA POD, HALVED
3 STAR ANISE

SERVE WITH SLICED APPLE ,
A FEW FRESH CRANBERRIES AND
A CINNAMON STICK ....
MMMMMMM....SMELLS SO GOOD!

CHOCOLATE FIG LAYER BARS

CRUST & TOPPING

1 cup brown sugar

1 cup butter

½ tsp. salt

½ tsp vanilla

1 ¾ cups rolled oats

1 ¾ cups flour

FILLING

8 oz. dried figs
stems removed and
finely chopped

1 cup sugar

½ cup chopped walnuts

½ cup hot water

¾ cup chocolate chips

for filling:
combine figs, sugar, nuts & water
in saucepan over medium heat
cook 15 minutes (stir often)
let cool

for crust:
cream butter & sugar
add salt, vanilla, oats & flour
mix until blended
spread 1/2 of mixture along bottom of greased 9 x 13 pan
spread filling evenly over dough
sprinkle chocolate chips over filling
crumble remaining dough over filling layer

bake at 350° for 30 minutes
allow to cool in pan
cut into squares

serve with vanilla ice cream and
drizzle of chocolate syrup

Queen Bee Rice Pudding

1 tsP. PuRe vaNilla ExtRact

3 1/2 cuP wHoLe MiLk

1/2 cuP shoRtgRaiN RiCe (ArBorio)

2 TBS. SugAr

PiNCH of sALt

3 TBS. HoNEY

1. BriNG miLk, RicE, suGAr, vaNiLLa and saLt To A BoiL iN mEDium sAucEPaN.

2. reDucE HeAt & siMMer (stirrinG often) untiL riCe iS tEnDeR & liQuiD aBsorBEd (Be PAtient!!) 20—25 miNutEs

3. REmovE fRom HeAt stiR iN HonEY (Let sTaND 5 Min.) (for extra—creamy pudding stir in 1/4 more milk)

4. diviDE AmonG PArfAit gLassEs & drizzLe wiTH HonEY

Sea Salt chocolate chip cookies

1 C + 2 TBS sugar

1 1/4 C brown sugar

2 C minus 2 TBS cake flour

1 2/3 C bread flour

sea salt

1 1/4 tsp. baking soda

2 large eggs

1 1/2 tsp. baking powder

2 1/2 sticks unsalted butter, softened

2 tsp. vanilla

16 oz. semi-sweet chocolate chips

1 1/2 tsp. salt

makes about 24 large cookies

sift dry ingredients
    into a bowl...*set* aside
cream butter and sugars til well mixed
    add eggs one at a time - *mix* well
        add vanilla

reduce mixer speed to low,
    add dry ingredients, *mix* til combined

    stir in chips
wrap dough in plastic and
        refrigerate for 24 hours

scoop golf ball size mounds
    of dough onto baking sheet
sprinkle lightly with sea salt
bake for 18-20 minutes
    in 350 degree preheated oven
cool for 5 minutes
    transfer to wire rack

1 cup sugar

2 sticks butter (room temperature)

1 egg yolk

3/4 cup chopped walnuts

2 cups flour

7 ounces
raspberry preserves

Raspberry Bars

grease 9 x 13 glass pan

preheat oven to 350

blend butter + sugar

with mixer or food processor til light + fluffy

add egg yolk + continue to mix

add flour 1/2 cup at a time til absorbed stir in walnuts

divide dough in 1/2

press half the dough into the bottom of the pan, coming up the sides slightly (it will be thin)

spread preserves over dough base (keeping away from edges)

crumble remaining dough over jam (no need to worry about covering completely)

bake at 350° for 40 minutes or until lightly brown (cool 15 minutes then cut)

AFFOGATO

SHAVE BITTERSWEET CHOCOLATE ON TOP

SPRINKLE OF NUTMEG

THEN ORANGE ZEST

1. *toss* two 12 oz. pkgs. *frozen mixed berries* with 2 TBS. *cornstarch* {let sit for 20 minutes}

2. divide berries among *6 custard cups*

3. *toss together*
1/2 C flour
1/2 C oats
1/2 C chopped walnuts
1/2 tsp cinnamon

4. *blend in* 6 TBS chilled butter (cut into cubes)

5. *evenly sprinkle* mixture over berries

Very Berry Crisp

place dishes

6. on baking sheet and bake for 10 min. at 425

reduce oven

7. to 350 and bake 30 more minutes

serve

with ice cream

apricots drenched in Chocolate &

(12 oz. dried apricots)

melt 1 TBS. butter + 16 oz. bag of
semi-sweet chocolate chips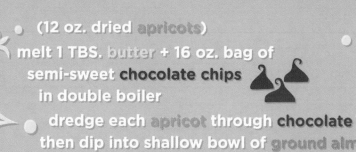
in double boiler

dredge each apricot through chocolate
then dip into shallow bowl of ground almonds
(coating both sides)

place on parchment lined baking sheet
and place in fridge for 15 minutes to set chocolate

(eat remainder of warmed chocolate with a big spoon + a big smile)

Dusted with almonds

santa is vegetarian
and trying to
lose a few...
maybe 10-15

Vegan Spice Cookies

1 1/2 c + 1 TBS flour
1 1/4 tsp ground ginger
1 tsp cinnamon
1/4 tsp ground cloves
1/4 tsp nutmeg
1 TBS cocoa powder
1/2 c vegan margarine
1/2 c brown sugar
1/4 c molasses
1 tsp baking soda
(dissolved in 1 1/2 tsp boiling water)
1/4 c sugar

whisk together:
flour, ginger, cinnamon, cloves,
nutmeg + cocoa in small bowl. set aside.
-beat together margarine + brown sugar. add molasses + mix.
-add 1/2 the flour mixture + combine well.
-add the rest of the flour mixture.
-chill covered for at least 1 hour. preheat oven to 325 degrees.
-spoon dough into 1 1/2" balls + roll in sugar
-bake 13-15 minutes, until surface starts to crack slightly.

DEar
SaNTa
+
ReiNDEER
XOX

mr. reindeer is vegan, of course.
he is drinking soy hot coca with
a vegan marshmallow...yes there
is such a thing, give it a google.

FABULOUS *figs*

mix together ½ cup plain greek *yogurt*…½ cup *mascarpone*…1 TBS *honey*…juice of 1/2 *lem*

cut 10 fresh *figs* in half…dollop with mixture & sprinkle with chopped *walnuts*

holiday
SPRITZERS

Pomegranate & sparkling water with lime

cheers!

I THINK I WAS BORN
A VEGETARIAN & OVER
THE YEARS I'VE DISCOVERED
THAT MY FAVORITE MEALS
ARE SIMPLE VEGGIE TOSS-UPS
USING LOTS OF COLORFUL
INGREDIENTS. I LIKE MEALS
THAT ARE SERVED IN ONE BIG BOWL WITH
A SIMPLE SALAD & MAYBE SOME RUSTIC BREAD —
NOTHING TOO FANCY — JUST HEARTY & COMFORTING.
I DON'T EAT MUCH DAIRY & PREFER MY EGGS TO
BE DISGUISED IN BAKED GOODS!
HOWEVER, I DO LOVE FETA
CHEESE & AGREE THAT
GENEROUS SPRINKLINGS
OF PARMESAN SHAVINGS
CAN ADD A LOT TO MOST
ANY DISH! ENJOY!!

THEY DRAW & COOK ™
Recipes Illustrated by Artists from Around the World

THE COLORFUL VEGETARIAN
by Salli S. Swindell

Conceived, designed and produced by
Studio SSS, LLC

STUDIO SSS, LLC
Nate Padavick & Salli Swindell
studiosss.com

*Visit *They Draw & Cook* to see over
3,000 more recipes illustrated by
artists from around the world!
theydrawandcook.com

*Also, check out *They Draw & Travel*
for hundreds of travel maps created
by artists from around the world.
theydrawandtravel.com

Made in the USA
Lexington, KY
01 August 2013